PHONICS CONNECTIONS

Finding Animals

by Wiley Blevins

capstone classroom

A big, green bug is on a stem. Can you see it?

A pretty, red bird is in a tree. Can you see it?

A tired lizard is resting on a wet rock. Can you see it?

A large, striped tiger is hiding in the tall grass. Can you see it?

A shy, scared crab went into a shell. Can you see it?

A white, furry rabbit rests in the snow.
Can you see it?

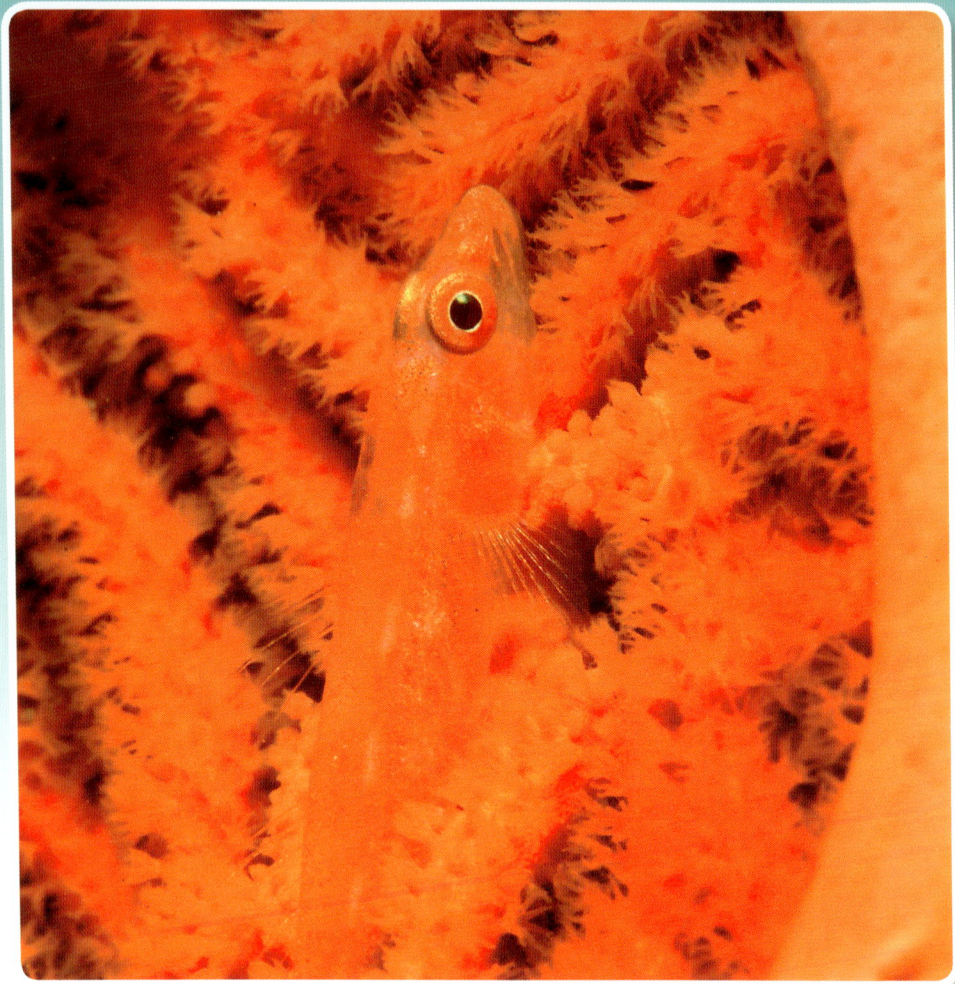

Can you see a small, red fish? Yes, I can see it!